THE YELLOW
HOTEL

THE YELLOW

HOTEL

POEMS

DIANE WALD

VERSE PRESS

AMHERST, MA

Published by Verse Press

Library of Congress Cataloging-in-Publication Data

Wald, Diane.
 The yellow hotel / by Diane Wald.– 1st ed.
   p. cm.
 ISBN 0-9723487-2-7 (alk. paper)
 I. Title.
 PS3573.A421147 Y45 2002
 811'.54–dc21

                           2002013583

Book designed and composed August, 2002, by J. Johnson.
Text is set in Electra. Display is set in Knockout.
Cover art by Michael Burkard.

Printed in Canada
9 8 7 6 5 4 3 2 1

FIRST EDITION

for Carey

of course and again

ACKNOWLEDGMENTS

"The Yellow Hotel," "Examining the Smallest Irritation," and "Working Off If" appeared in *The American Poetry Review*.

"The Rectangular Slot..." and "Molecules of the Air..." appeared in *Fence*.

"Hell Money," "Lily Pollen Stains," "The Smallest Breeze," and "green dress, top button" appeared in *Skanky Possum*.

"Raft of Self-Portraits..." appeared in *The Hat*.

"As a Heart of New Pushed Hardness..." appeared in *Verse*.

"the conversation" appears online in *Mudlark*.

"voices of the dinosaurs" appears online in *How2*.

"Family Values" appeared in *Calapooya*.

"how we were happy in spain..." appears online in *Web del Sol*.

• • •

Love, thanks, a wisteria pod, and a wren to Bobby Dogwood and Dr. M.P.B. Vienna for living in and with so many of my poems.

And profound gratitude to Matthew Zapruder, Brian Henry, and Lori Shine at Verse Press for their life-sustaining enthusiasm for this book, and to J. Johnson for his brilliant design work.

CONTENTS

A FORWARD VOICE

Well I have seen everything you have done and just as always I am enchanted by it.

Your beautiful taste in floors and flowers.

The tall palm needs to be repotted you know there is no other way around it.
Also the small one.

Am I talking to myself?

It occurs to me that there are two ways to poetry, not two ways of poetry though
that may also be. Two ways vital, two and a lot of others. The *deep internal
personal* and—the *sustaining*. When these two come together there is yes for
me yes for you, always yes you feel it.

It occurs to me that the *sustaining* can be learned or absorbed by great *desiration*
(desiring), and that the *deep internal personal* must be released. Before it.

At times this can be released by money.

How else to release it.

I am having trouble again with breath, that is part of it. Going down the stairlike
ramp in the Picasso museum in Paris I had the same problem. A coolgreen
corner was there.

I hid. I enjoyed it.
Profound desiration.

I find a slip of paper I have obviously importantly saved that says "Condemned
Unit Armory" and have no idea what it means.

Suddenly I see you are increasingly interested in Spanish which does not
surprise me. We are going to Spain. But you are not going to Spain and still you
like it.

One way to release it is to spend the morning walking. With something to speak
into. For this you must not be afraid to go out.

No number you can call, and the shoes are not strange. Cypress as either a
          beautiful book
or
the breath of the beleaguered.
I AM FREE TO SAY TO SHOW THESE THINGS.

Thank you they are beautiful.

I am not condemned to the armory: I release it.

A voice comes forward from the background. The summer barrage of
          coincidence begins.

Do not be afraid of the sun, though it is damaged. The sun has a heart and the
          heart is pulled open. Let
sun's heart deny
a valentine: two amendments
to one mind.

How to release it and achieve *sustenation* (sustaining): at the fold of the
notecard from last August a drop of liquid has seeped in and made a Rorschach:

two beetles dancing or two
beetles dancing upside
-down, or
a thin-lipped man with
cross-sections of pineapple, or microscopic
pincers (pinching) and also
a dangling brow, a
possibility
of — "It could
rain, I suppose, and then
I would not be afraid."

Repeated repeated repented repleted reported repotted reputed
reposed.

I wished I had found the book, which contains a secret. Then everyone
arrived at once.
The book was called *A Lemon and a Star,* but I cannot find it.
He entered the bedroom at 12:28 a.m. I'd been asleep, it's true. Head of
        electric fan bent down, which he
immediately noticed.

Turning. The small air.

Somehow there was breeze on one side of the sheet not the other.

Maybe that can release it.

"If he shot himself in the heart..." How could he. And they said he only looked
        like he was sleeping.

Here you can read in peace and coolness with a strawberry plate. The barker
does not bark. The horner does not horn. There's a leaf already falling that will
help you release it, then sustain. You or the leaf will not drift to the ground

for a long time.

What was ever done to us that we've not also done.

The soundless sound of the pen
moving in unison with itself the pen
and the trucks moving by in the city.

The same ridiculous body in a clean white room.

I WANTED TO STOP YOUR HEART.

Tilt your head back.

I won't hurt you.

THEN I REMEMBERED

there was more to it than that, than desiration and sustenation, ha!

I envisioned a lot of this during the t.v. show on volcanoes. Two people,
volcano experts, *vulcanologists*, were so unafraid
they went nearly into the heart of exploding mountains
to take pictures. But in Japan they were killed. Surreal photos showed them
in heat-resistant space suits of some kind, walking the rim of the heat, with raging
fires and pyroclastic flow
all around them. Oddly
the footage also showed the man
setting up his cameras and saying, "If I died tomorrow
I would be happy,"
and he did.

Sustenation everywhere. Also precognition, and, we hope,
therefore,
a truth.

Something about the fabulously beautiful, sensual, rich-faced gladiolus
that nobody really likes. A funeral flower, perhaps, at least that's the reason
usually given, but I think there's more to it. A bit like my eternal trying to discern
why one person bothers me and another doesn't, even though
the one who bothers is *seemingly* always doing "the right thing."

Seemingly.

"Well shouldn't a poem have a theme?" she said. She was
pushy
about this.
I find this difficult to answer.

The little Chinese pug at the beach who slept on his person's back. Now there's
a theme.
He wore a little harness
not connected to anything.

I keep painting. Well I don't exactly, but it's a head thing. A *paintful* head.

This huge bowl of winding cactus fronds which it seems would be impossible to
        re-pot.
Now there's a theme. One could wear gloves, I suppose, but still...
it *seems* difficult.

On Saturday night I ate a much-too-large slab of onion by mistake.
I thought only one side of it was thick.
A mistake I keep making.

Early this morning (two a.m.) I find your e-mail about a dream.
If you have really fallen down into the telephone as you say we may never find you.
This would disturb me unceasingly—not finding you, I mean.

Get to know
the damaged parts
the cold ankles
let everyone see
let them examine
everything
up close
in blinding light
you just sit there
let them do it.

Now that I've ceased trying to find out your answers

There is a pocket of air behind your winsomest voice
that smells of the second white violet of spring.

LILY POLLEN STAINS

1.

I thought I heard you come in the front door; I could tell your hands were stained
with lily pollen—it doesn't come off. Yesterday
I had some all over the thumb edge
of my left hand.

It wasn't you, but it sounded like it.

Also there were, so magically, three sprigs of fresh dill in the bouquet; it looked like
Queen Anne's Lace
in a way. Who would ever think
of including dill with flowers?

The flowers that arrived even before our stay at the yellow hotel.
The flowers that imbibed some sense of our growing season, the one in our heads.
The flowers that took our hearts out to breakfast at the table by the window
       on which you insisted.
The flowers in the window the flowers in the pillow the flowers in the showerhead
       that did not work.

This is not certainly to say that everything was perfect.
Certainly I made some unfortunate remarks, am still making them.
And you, let's face it, were not at your best,
but of course you do have that intestinal thing and who could stand it.

When you embarrassed me I tried to be understanding.

In last night's dream I tried to drill a hole with a hand drill at eye level
in a tall green door, the green of garden furniture.
I could tell that my brother was behind that door,
but I could not get in to save him.
He wore a white shirt, as he often does. And then yesterday, after the dream,
M said he (brother) had mailed him

a box full of treasures
and I have to admit I was a little jealous
since he (brother) does not send me
treasures
any more.

These treasures consisted of small things he (brother) had made, drawn, painted, or
found.
Or written.
And I wonder why—or if—

why or if
why
if
whyif. That's all I wonder
but it takes up the better part of the morning, although not in an annoying way.
I am learning
that men almost never apologize.
And I am learning about the dream and the brother and
my goddamned critical nature.

That wasn't the only dream however. Next I had a ridiculous piled-up hairdo
that looked like Marge Simpson's
but wasn't blue. This hairdo prevented me
from trying on a dress I wanted,
which obviously would make one think the dream had a THEME

of vanity, but I wish it were only as simple as that.

The moon last night was as close to full as possible and startled us
on the boat. Many of the islands
could not be identified
except by one man who joined us
to point out the very old island sanitarium
that was now used to house the homeless.
Lights shone brightly
from every window. In my mind I called it

Dignity Island, then realized "D.I." was my nickname,
Di.
Also we passed the huge steel sculpture I immediately did not like
and C pointed out to me that it had to be cordoned off
so kids wouldn't skateboard on it and therefore we couldn't
exactly appreciate its glory. When the sun shone through the fencing
just about the whole effect of the four steel slabs
was ruined.
And he was right.

I awoke with a backache because of all this dreaming and boating.

I do like the blue color of Marge Simpson's hairdo however.

2.

Jackrabbit caused a ruckus when Coyote spied him.
Together they searched the shelves for their favorite film.

O piper-pied lopperstam.
And the pleasure in that one.

Try to write a poem in six seasons.
If this means non-nonsense words to you, that's fine.

For the most part only girls were born in that family.
And I noticed only daughters on the boat last night.

Every time you hear her name or her mother's name you change faces.
I wish you could believe me.

It's taken all these years for the large-leafed wallpaper to fade
and yet it was torn from the walls in the later '50s.

Backache as symbol.
Backache as tiny yellow toadstool.

For a while we talked about tallness.
Two people on the beach at dusk, aware of single couplets.

3.

The torturous days of
nothin' doin'
are over. And this morning
Lucinda Williams singing "look for my joy." Why don't you
set out to do what you must in your own world and not worry about the rest.

For example one could easily start (or end) the day by writing
a poem that ends (or begins) in the word *you.*

It would not be difficult
if that's what makes you happy.

I hear a chain-link fence in your voice that has nothing to do
with the fact that I cannot replace the dried leaves around the edge of this picture
        frame until I find the rubber cement
which you say you have not taken.

I'd like to tell you another dream but I don't want you to get the idea
all my dreams are unpleasant—quite the contrary. Nevertheless two nights ago I
        dreamed of P's house,
where there was about to be
some kind of wedding, possible hers. And possibly she was marrying the woman
she sat on the couch with. I thought I could do them a favor
by sewing a ripped fancy pantsuit I found hanging on the back of the door,
but it turned out to belong to someone else entirely: a stranger
from Eastern Europe
who was panicky about the crazy way
I'd sewn the pieces together
and also she was nervous that I'd lost the heavy coins
in the inside vest pocket,
but I hadn't.

All of a sudden there was my mother (very small) in a store
standing all alone with a little blue handkerchief
over her head. I was driving around
in a Lincoln, had trouble parking, the car kept changing.

I wonder if there's a little something going on I don't want to know about.

Possibly this feeling was presaged
by a pondful, actually a crowded crowd,
of Canada geese. It looked as if
they could not move
all floating there
in a huge clump.
I'd never seen anything like it before: the whole surface
of the pond was geese.

In the end you know I really want to know
want to know want to know want to
know
(o know o no)
about it all.

If there is something going on I really do want to know about it.

WORKING OFF IF

He says if the natural world is natural next week—meaning *his* natural world of course and there's no way to tell about that—if the natural world is natural then there won't be any reason to worry will there and she says *yes*. She means *no* and it is taken so and she appears to be going back to her fine work and it appears that everything is normal. And then later when they are alone he says if the genuine attitude of *not*-knowing weren't real—but of course it is, he comments, and what can she say—if that weren't real then maybe if all the other things fell in place— but of course they couldn't, he comments, and she agrees in part at least and she says so, briefly—but just if all of that were true, maybe...

HELL MONEY

The seagull carries something that looks like a key
and the cloud involves something that looks like a door
and still there's no resolution.

Not that we were particularly sullen, not that.
I fell into a deep sleep. Feel into a dip slip.
And I was wishing to celebrate something—I forget what.

That's a lie. I know full well.
I wanted to celebrate something, cerebrate something

with you.

But because of the noise of the airplanes,
because of the cat's nails making marks on the hardwood floor,
because of the persistent stomach discomfort,
because you are learning the harmonica,
because of the very fact that I wanted to celebrate,
there was an assassination

an assassination of intent
assassination of joy-mood
assassination of opportunity
assassination of abstract pleasure,

and so I was unable to discuss it.

I understand that really no one here is at all in favor
of sabotage.

Nevertheless it goes on and I'm sad.

I remember snow
and the little lemur's grieving for his brother

in the forest on television—the look on his face that explained
his nerve-end understanding
of inevitability.

And on the subject of those people on whom we often disagree,
I'm sorry I do not like him or her or both of them together.

Perhaps it just isn't the right time for all this.
I don't want to start something else.

Chapultepec, your mother is calling.

She had to be highly amplified
and even then we could not hear her.
We left the recorder running with the sound turned off.

We left prettypaper hell money we bought in Chinatown
as an offering to appease the ghosts.

We jumped into a grave that had just been dug
and did the fox-hole fox-trot.

It was enough,
eventually. Then I slept.

What can you do now you are so tired.

THE SMALLEST BREEZE

Aspirin at 3 a.m. in the comfort of aspen leaves.
A boot for you, the one foot.
Eiderduck helped me drive.

No I don't know what you went through;
you won't tell me. A sawdust documentary—
cedar, I think. And various other silences
docile in the moonlight.

In the moonlight a tame woodchuck, maybe two,
eye-to-eye with me under the round redwood table turned grey.
A fly on their little grey face, walking back into sleep.

Like a dream the sound of paper tearing.
I go repair it.

AUTUMN RAIN

Ideas in bed
and how they fled.

Outside in the rain at five a.m. this morning a mis-marked skunk: U-shaped white
design on his black head and no other white except a white-tipped tail. No wide
white stripe. Now he's resting under C's truck, probably licking himself like a cat.

Pattering pattering patterning and always looking
for the right shoes.

Some people walk right up to you and put their faces close.

The sunflower stalks need to be cut back, also the roses. The echinacea has
all turned black: black towers sunspires daisy-faces everywhere. And the
woman who delivered a package last week, I saw her looking closely at the
garden. She picked up something from the flagstones. I will never know what it
was.

There's a little thunder now, a warm fine rain. All week this itchy feeling.

I had nothing. No part of it.
A scream in the eastern corridor.
A black tuck in the back of the dress.
Ominous?

Second day of rain. Some people can't type. Some people pick at the keyboard,
and at life. And why do people look so different day to day? The same people?
Something they ate? "Within the limits of HTML," he said, and I remembered
searching furiously through the Paris streets for the correct *gare*.

My husband does not sleep well and this house is noisy so you cannot do much
when he is sleeping. Someone called for him, but only asked for him, didn't even
say one hello to me. "She's just that way," is what the excuse would be.

I AM CHANGING THE BACKGROUND COLORS.

This will be the weekend that so many blind things will see.

Light travels down the spine to the soul, which is nowhere visible.

And I suffer over and over from a feeling of being left out. One would think one could shine simply by one's lights and be seen, but the truth is sometimes one's lights serve only to illuminate others.

I am sure this resonates to childhood, when I was constantly deceived. Put into the car expecting to go to the store and ending up in the dentist's chair. Told that my father had some kind of flu, when he was really in the hospital from a heart attack. Told that I was loved, told that I was homely.

Now I have two secrets, neither of which makes me happy.

HAVING LOST THE HABIT

Wild beings return to the burned-out forest
gingerly, lifting each paw
with care.

I try so distinctly to remember your hands.

BRING IN SCIENCE, DRESSED AS RAIN

Try not to be cowered
by the vastness of fact.

Just now the lichen on that wriggly branch.
That snail I picked off the rose leaf and threw across the road.

Or that actress, the one we loved, now dead of thinness,
or those most often difficult five-letter words, like *Diane*.

Everything has become
what it least expected: this solitude for example, a queen.

In no way do the noises correspond
to the beginning or end of images, necessarily.

Can one arm be warmer than the other
on the same body?

We put things inside our hunger
and the hunger turns into satiety. Just like that.

THE DEVOTION SCHOOL

A young blond man asks us on the street if we know where to find "The Devotion School." We don't, but he doesn't want to believe it, and we have to tell him several more times. He can't give any further information about the place—what it's connected to, what's going on there—but seems desperate to know where it is. We cannot help him.

M said he was trying to "write when he thought he was bored," and I meant to ask him about it, but forgot. A curious assignment, which implies that thinking one is bored doesn't necessarily mean one is. Or at least that's one permutation. Also he uses a great phrase about a typo of some kind, "a grammatical hole." Maybe more than a typo, and something deserving this phrase-making.

I wish we had been able to direct the young man to The Devotion School.

At least that's one permutation.

Perhaps there he would have learned the devotion one lover gifts another? If so, what a delightful young man.

Of course god might have been involved, but it just didn't look that way from the face of that asker.

The Devotion School might have something to do with writing. Or the way C kissed me at least fifteen times around the face before he had to go. Or flowers, definitely flowers. Self-devotion, yes, another possibility.

I would like to enroll in this Devotion School myself.

Does everyone know what it means except me?

DON'T BE CAREFUL

I could get away with this if I could.
And in the morning light go nowhere.

I am up and around now and the clouds count six,
one looming over the cemetery neatly.

As if all the adjectives were gold, as if light hit
the faces of loved ones without pain.

Or painlessly, adverb, self-consciously a dream.
I could lick all your fingers; I'm afraid to.

But really it's more like *like*.
In the same way a metaphor like me would lick them.

FAMILY VALUES

"The spider has learned me art."
Howard Finster (1916-2001)

I have a dream that my mother marries Howard Finster and we all live in Paradise Gardens having visions together before dinner and eating only vegetables we've grown ourselves, but of course letting some of the artichokes go to seed so we can enjoy looking at their gorgeous big thistles. Since my mother is a widow when she marries Howard my brother and I don't have to call him dad and he calls me Miss Diane and my brother Little Robert and he lets us help design the open birdcage made of bicycle frames and refrigerator shelves and we both drop out of school in the second grade although we have access to Howard's fine library of the many books sent to him by admirers. My mother seems happy enough although I never imagined she'd marry again. Are these two contented together? What do they see in each other? My brother and I believe she married Howard for his fabulous plywood smile and because he promised he'd make something out of us. He has. He walks with us out to a pond he has built in the back of Paradise Gardens and we sit in the hot Georgia sun on the hot Finster mosaics of Elvis and some other American heroes. "Kids," Howard says, "I'm gettin' on in years and so's your mama. Pretty soon you're gonna hafta take over this here artistic business and make it your own." He reaches into a knapsack he's brought along and takes out two finely carved wooden crowns—one encrusted with seashells and one with striped marbles. "These here are your own holy headdresses," Howard says, and places one on each of our heads. "Now go and be people, for I must return to the visionary planet where I was born." Little Robert and I discuss the weight and beauty of our crowns for a while, then we notice how Howard's disappeared from his chair. We're good talkers, my brother and I, but we really can't imagine how we'll ever tell our mom.

[for Bobby Dogwood]

EXAMINING THE SMALLEST IRRITATION

In the forest the limbs are criss-crossed back into time, as far as you can see, and I see no reason to say *one* there when I can say *you*. I tried again and again to let everyone know

that informality was queen. King?

L said thanks for talking about sexism but really what I was doing was talking about talking. And I know if I had a way to follow these limbs criss-crossed back into time...

I would be holier.

I would be holier and have written more, written better. Now next week a man will come and talk to us about a party. Aboutaparty. His name is S and I don't think he gets it:

nobody wants a party.

At least not the kind he's thinking of. Nevertheless we will be cooperative up to our comfort levels—ha! Suddenly I realize it must have been a day like this

when we first went north to the gardens.

In those days we could afford very little, and I bought perhaps fifteen tiny pots of cacti, many of which survived and thrived for some years.

Would you worry if you knew I was talking about you? Aboutyou.

Probably you would not exactly worry but would be angry. I used to try to find ways to talk to you, like letters, but in the end it was the letter from you that hurt the most.

You had no skill in letters.

Yet you faded away quite quickly, in the scheme of things. I can't say that about the other *you*, who's with me still, whose face I touched last night in a dream.

That *you* is a curious comfort.

It might have stopped raining enough today to take a bike ride. Theotheryou. I can be fairly sure at this point that no one will go with me.

MOLECULES OF THE AIR ARE MOVING

suddenly there's a note on the inside of the door although no one's been there
       but you

i believe in the holy placebo

i am not perfect god knows

i don't read as much as i used to

i'm not so fussy

what does it mean when you say to someone *take this flower you need it*
what does it mean when someone else says *i knew where she was coming from*
what does it mean that you wonder what these things mean

i wish i had more notebooks i wish i had yours

THE FEAR AS THE HEIGHT OF FOLLY

1.

If I could see where I am going, would I go there?

Morning light ambles down the raining street like a grey horse.

In all ways but one I am a wanderer: I do not like to travel.

2.

Just before dawn, the porchlight still on, the streets golden plaster.

Broken giant sunflower stalks, peony bushes turning yellow and silver.

The mechanic who came to start the car stepped on the last of the cosmos.

3.

None of these occurred as truly as the dream of my husband.

When I reach out for him in the night he is there without knowledge of the dream.

This has happened so many times. Do you know when I dream of you?

4.

The ordinary terrors that vine around my lungs.

Thinking what I do not need to think, in the face of the world's wonders.

And because of all this I reject what once I desired.

5.

That young girl with the heavy body, she's afraid too.

My friend said she let him pass through the doorway first.

And yesterday her eyes: pearls rubbed free of luster, mean pearls, so tired.

6.

The woman who won't leave her past is afraid; you call her *mother.*

She thinks the past is a town, or a church, or a window.

She has grown so small she must laugh in the dress store at sizes.

7.

We argue about his thinness, which is relevant to nothing.

One time he parked the car in New York so expertly it made me cry.

Later in a novel I based a fish dinner on that.

8.

It was not Mexico, though we were there, when the pain looked on.

Curanderas in the square, and their merciless victims.

Occlusion of the veritable arteries, enwashment of the ovarian ear.

9.

Nor was it in Paris. I hid books there, and in the Alhambra.

Never think you know more than you know, about Spain.

On the Calle Nervosa a million and six mariachis who feel the cold.

10.

Pushing thumbs into my body to check for the fear.

Pushing thumbtacks into fence posts: *Lost Fear, Please Call If Found.*

Pushing back into the womb, where the biggest fears began.

sentences for parsing

i am just waking up to my eyes which waking is very pretty

the shadow is an ant on the other side of the white window shade

does the sign say *sale* or are the letters all mixed up in the box of sight

when the anarchist plumber discusses componentarianism with my husband
	i am not there

i believe i dreamed again of the pajamas of the peregrine falcon

she married with a dowry of postmodern conveniences

the plastic surgeon has removed her desire

i investigate ephemeroptera as well as the cagey viburnum

the large polar bear which i found in the neighbor's garbage is often named edward

if you quickly hand someone a large white bear their arms automatically close
	around it

don't worry about the plural possessive please

there are finite considerations regarding the barber's final customer

most anteaters like cashews

an afternoon thunderstorm cools the pink tree's blossoms and knocks them down

'your toenail again on the floor' is not a sentence

nor 'the careful arrangement of scatter pins on a lapel'

IF YOU HAVE A COMPLICATED IDEA

It spreads to the torso,
usually.

Grackle ate a squirrel yesterday, one flattened on the road.
Grackle was grateful, not dimished by this service.

Our bodies are half-a-hundred years old.

A pause after the sound that you can't hear (the pause)
and a pause before doing nothing (that you can't know).
I pause when I see you because of this vast love.

Only the roots have supported the plant; without them
it topples over. Everyone
knows this.

And yet the stars have no roots (you can't see them)
and the man has no roots (you can't know).
He is sleeping now.
He is breathing.

will it come and will it come at an inopportune time

and i have resolved to say nothing to you about itineraries or flowers or white
       dictionaries
and i have resolved to say nothing to say nothing no nothing at all

(not understanding the southern as they say accent
i thought he said *i would like to go home and put my hot toes in a bucket of eyes*)

when i was crossing the street i had a white hat
when i got to the other side i had two white hats a corncob pipe and a green
       feather

he takes his white vitamins with beer in the summer
and changes his name quite often to angela and peter
as peter is fisher of men he remembers from childhood churches
and angela he just loves her just loves her to pieces

i regress to the museum with the ship models in the basement
you know the one
no rothko i regret to say
i dreamed there in the library and restroom
where the art deco lamps shone flat white against grey-white walls
who do you think was there in my dreams but the infamous toy donkey of new jersey

a spy in your eye

i feel i have entered a wide white space and you are there and not there
there and not there
i feel i cannot tell and i do not wish to hurt you

the conversation

the conversation did not go well
i said the conversation did not go well
the conversation did not go well although a lot was said
the woman in the war-world office said to the soldier please send me flowers
the soldier said no
the soldier said please tell my mother i am
sad the mother said i am watching the anniversary of the end of the war
       in vietnam on tv it looks so nice there
the mother said the people are pretty the lights are all shining why were you so
       afraid

the reporter said i cannot report what was said it did not go well
the little hawk said i was flying right over the bombs
the butterfly said i was about to be immortalized in embroidery when the
       embroiderer was vaporized
the vaporized woman said no one is listening
the conversation did not go well

please you could hear in the background please please please please
but you could not hear it up front
up front there was rudeness up front there were a million rules
don't say it this way don't say it that way a million rules at least
and the conversation was not going well

the woman in the wide white hat said i must go home now i cannot stay
the woman in charge of the woman in the wide white hat said no you cannot
the man married to the woman who wanted to leave wanted to have a
       conversation
with the woman in charge of all white hats but was told he could not
it wasn't appropriate
so he talked to the woman he was married to but she was listening to a strange
       white bird
and did not hear him
in that sense he did not feel the conversation had gone very well

the bird said no we've all got the willies
we will not be building nests this year
there will be no more baby birds for the crows to prey on
there will be no more baby birds to fall out of the nest

the birds said we have the chills we need warm coats we need little blue mufflers
the man said i cannot hear the birds i don't know what they are saying
they should stop trying to talk to me now and go build some nests
the conversation just did not go well

the old woman said i am dying i want to talk to the birds
the doctor said here let us just remove this white spot from your skin
the woman said no that is a wide white hat that is not a spot and i want to die
          with my white spot intact
the doctor began again to say no and was interrupted by the bird
who flew in the hospital window and was shooed out by the broom of the janitor
in no sense did the conversation go well

the woman in the war-world office and the soldier and the mother
the reporter the little hawk the butterfly the embroiderer the vaporized woman
the woman in the wide white hat and the woman in charge of her and the man
          married to her

the bird who had the willies the baby birds the crows the man who could not
          hear them
the old woman the doctor the bird who flew in the hospital window the janitor

all are deaf all can speak all are deaf all are sorry

BEFORE THE OPENING

G wants to go with me, but can't be sure of the time; must get a babysitter for Z; can I call her at five? Maybe even H will go, she says. At five when I call she's not home and there's no babysitter and H says it isn't even five yet, but it is. I don't know why he wants to argue about this. I go alone on the subway with my memories of a hundred years. When I get to South Station the stars are very near for the city; I get disoriented looking up at them and cross the wrong street at first. A fancy building. Lobby palms. Guard at the door friendly; gives me a little tag to wear. Inside warm, almost endless ceilings; later H comments that it keeps the noise way down; maybe he's saying it was too quiet, I can't be sure. For me a relaxing day, the first in a month; almost no interruptions. I know this will change, so I wear a black sweater. I impale a valise on my heart, into which I can stuff excess grief.

AT THE OPENING RECEPTION

S only catches my eye; later G asks if I'd said hello to him, as if it were an obligation—as if we would gain something from it. I'm already getting angry; it seems she is here to preen. One of G's two pieces is sitting on the floor, but the one I really like, the clay "Buddhette," is mounted on a stand, imposing. I remember last year for my birthday when she gave me a beautiful clay water glass with a squared-off mouth that made it hard to drink from, and my anger changes to sadness. C and I bump into N, who is charming; as always he has an amusing story—this time about a man who goes to a hypnotist so he can get up early, but then he gets up early and stares at his coffee mug until eleven o'clock. If I had money I'd buy the fish triptych, the skeletons showing through x-ray-like fish, but large, larger than flounder, and underwater-murky and in rough frames. Or I'd buy CG's large abstract piece which she says is evolving or about evolving. C's wine tastes pleasant, surprisingly. C, good-hearted, tries to be jolly with B, but B slides away from us looking confused and pained. Every day B got worse, eventually saying poor S. was the "devil," asking me to make a phone call to an ordinary office for him as if there were some immoral international plot in progress which would involve him if he made the phone call himself. Now he accuses me of being hyperbolic, which of course I am. A student has a small painting about "guppy-sucking," which many of us seem to like, or at least the title. C and I go off with G and H and Z in their old lemon Toyota. The cold streets are pleasant to me and riding in the back seat is fun. G continues to make strange jokes; I become increasingly silent. Nevertheless I know she likes me, which only makes things worse.

AT THE RESTAURANT AFTER THE OPENING

Z is drawing a hippo on a placemat simply because I asked; she gives me this drawing, which makes G mad. G would never admit that, but it's the same as when L is nice to E in a way that perhaps I should be ("should" as the demon), and this upsets me—not so much that she says things I wish no one would say, but that she says them nicely. I cannot blame L; G cannot blame me. The hippo drawing is perfect, a hippo floating in a lake, and Z like a film director, drawing all in one take. Also Z gives me a lion with wings and a portrait of the two llamas I requested, which she has signed in block letters, the signature as big as the llamas. Humorously she has placed the llamas' eyes way down on their noses; C tries to correct this. I tell Z how there was a spot on the one llama's back and she dutifully, humorously, draws it on both. They're looking splendid. I want to tell her about the conversations I had with those llamas, but there is no time. I could never tell L that; she would emanate doubt and "should." Or perhaps I misjudge L; it's all I can do now. H sits back quietly when he feels I am angry with G for inquiring about the billboard for the twentieth time. I'd asked her not to do that, and felt she should not ask, should not. I feel C's hand on my knee; he knows I am sad. He asks me for a kiss, which I give, and G is mocking. H's blue shirt is electric blue. Z's dress is black-and-white animal spots and her blond hair is braided. The lack of one thing, the love of another. I know G is troubled, but I cannot help her. I know this same scene will take place a thousand times, with the animals changed and the clothing, but not the sorrow.

RAFT OF SELF-PORTRAITS, SEA OF DELIBERATION

1. Ornamental Grass

Begin by starting here on a long walk, with voices.

Listen to where the red "N" is.

I am a thin muffin on a tin plate of fat ones, with raisins.

The raisins I ate yesterday, in the broccoli pasta, were surprisingly good.

I go around picking up little things from all the tables.

In 1931, many years before my birth, my twin was born in Kulxshek.

2. The Bold-Faced Lie

I more or less knew what was going on all the time.

I ate the watermelon, ate the small ragged pie

to keep up my strength for the long discussions that were to come.

I took a long walk in the high grasses and felt nauseous about the crickets

many of whom had been vaporized in the drought.

However you would never know it by looking at them, curious beings.

O honey, I love you, I heard one of them say.

3. Magic in Visible Veins

I wonder if I will ever see her again, the me with the muffins.

She looked down at her legs, saw them shrivel like the crickets.

She was variously afraid and not afraid.

It was somewhere in Nevada where we first met

after knowing each other for about three years.

There the town fathers played the slot machines.

Three white pebbles between each set of toes, held tight.

It's the silence she always liked best there's no getting around it.

4. One Night Watching the Red Planet Mars

Suddenly it became okay to do anything, in spite of popular opinion.

In later years this applied to poetry.

One has to be stealthy.

Possibly imbibe a lot of fruit

and give away silver.

Whatnots.

Anything.

As long as it's silver not gold.

There are stains on the blouses that never come out you have not to care.

5. Questions from the Hairnet

Will you say anything?

Will you just say anything?

No that's not it. No tit.

Does the lizard face one way

and then the other?

Is all this necessary and are they watching you through the window?

It did seem as if they'd seen.

6. A Little Disappointment Goes a Long Long Way

I could have told you he wouldn't like it he never does.

It doesn't have anything to do with you.

I just wish he would stop saying everything's all right

when clearly everything isn't always it couldn't be.

His pedicure is all right according to him too.

I wonder if B. remembers that Irish Setter scrabbling for a foothold on the
        linoleum floor

next to the shiny white washer.

When he was a baby that washer would lull him to sleep.

7. Shawls Are Not As Good As Sweaters in My Opinion

It's just that you have to hold on to them and can't really use your hands for
    anything else.

I wish you were here right now.

The voice of the man next door with the brain disease: finally

I understand the sounds he makes are rhythms of comfort,

sorry.

Just like the card game I play by myself sometimes is a gauge of looseness.

I never win when I'm uptight.

8. Beautiful Ox in the Dream

He turned around in the street in front of the furniture store and all eyes were on him.

In the gutter of the house next door a little tree is growing just fine among the bird
    nests.

I haven't seen Vireo yet this morning, but he's out there.

Suddenly I remember chatting with the anesthetist about Neruda and how freeing
    that was.

And my whole history of you.

My whole history with you.

Whole histories of you which when in hollowing moods cause huge comfort.

9. A NOISE Directly from the Rising Moon

I asked who said never leave poetry the way you found it.

Especially when several of us say we're having trouble reading novels.

Suddenly the house is shiny and the cat's afraid: potted plants in moonlight on
the balcony.

One: a shooting-star hoya.

Two: a spider caught in my hair, lowering herself on a silver filament in front of
my glasses.

Two: my husband now in New Hampshire studying spiders.

Never before have I heard such a noise from the moon!

as recently as now

so exceptional a net
the anode spinning like a penny on ice
its orbit out of conscience
all capes and traces
bereft
i am aging
i fight to move
i dream the ukulele slave (liquor between the depths and these hopes)
the vacuum's detective
night medicine lost and floating up nameless in a
bowl
of white water
the mate of toast
listing slightly left
when marriage vibrated
like the dial on a gas meter
to care was cream then
was berries
dolls swerving between shores of girls' desires
woolly vacillation
and proofs unprovided
that the chocolate hedgehog wasn't real
i am your van
you have provided me to the keywords
and now they understand me
no one openly cries
no one wing against the darkness
a fee belonging to someone else
sketches of it
foam and coffee and power a-hum in the wires
town between cushions and trolleys
our last veneration of flight

THE YELLOW HOTEL

It probably always has something to do with the typeface, and this time also the two photos I forgot to put in the envelope—one with him holding the circle of grass I have in my hair in a different picture—

those two photos
have something to do with it too. And a dead bee

inside the back window of the car. The Panama hat that C won't wear.

I hear a certain tone of voice sometimes and I hate to recognize its unbearable sweetness. It's like the first time I recognized *metaphor* as something I could do—I was a child reading

a child's book, and that inclination leapt out at me

in the guise of a pile of mashed potatoes going down to *bandage*

some bad feelings in the little girl's stomach

in that book. Mashed potatoes! Well not strictly metaphor you say, but I say close enough. And this weekend I read that same book again, having looked for it on an internet search through an out-of-print-book store in Illinois and I was still

enchanted. This matter is time consuming, enchantment; this matter is critical.

Today the customer (40-year-old man) and the cashier (30-year-old woman) in the convenience store laughed and exchanged loud sexual innuendoes

as if I weren't there. And also a religious fanatic approached me as I was getting into my car in the rain in the parking lot near the mall where I bought a new iron and he said, to get my attention, *you look like a fine woman,* and I replied not too kindly but not nastily either.

I was trying. But I didn't want to get into it.

In his arms he had a pile of damp books and I could see the word *enlightenment* on the spine of one of them.

Still it never crossed my mind he had any to offer,

although I suppose he might have.

The yellow hotel was empty to capacity and that's why we enjoyed it.

The ballroom danced out over the sea.

There were fifty-nine rooms

with private baths. (In the brochure they left the "s" off so it sounded like one for all those rooms.) Our shower head was broken

but we almost didn't mind.

I must say (as C would say) *I must say* a strangeness visited me that second morning. The day before C had seen a fox on the hotel grounds. I remembered I thought that L had seen a fox in Rhode Island also, or someone had.

Anyway it might be the strangeness came from a dream, or possibly the large late meal we ate in the hotel dining room where we opened our presents (his a wrought iron spider on a web, mine a pink and lavender rainbowed green smooth fluorite heart)

or possibly a little medication I was taking for an infection, or probably all of those and more.

Or morel, a kind of mushroom
I'm not sure I've ever tasted. Depression

can be contagious—in my case, and sometimes in yours. I think there was a full moon that night. I dreamed

of T, fuller of face than he really is, a puzzle. He was sitting at a table in a library and I knew he was famous. People would be coming for autographs, and he was getting ready.

Later in the dream I was taken away from this area/building in a sort of pony or ox cart (like the one in *The Paradine Case*, which intrigued me) and I was in the back—the cargo area—of the cart, and looking out the back I saw a vast city, a wonderful detailed city, full of lights (daytime) and fabulous clean friendly buildings.

In another dream A appeared oddly with her mouth sliding down the side of her face, and this after W and I had just discussed her dualities. Also I kept my favorite cat in a guitar case for a while and also someone stole my purse. This purse-stealing dream (or sometimes purse-losing) is becoming

recurrent. Also T's brother and sister appeared as a romantic couple somehow and there was something very funny about the stairway banister that I forget now.

Anyway this familiar strangeness came along.

The surf was pounding outside the yellow hotel bedroom window where we slept very well. I was aware during the night that C wanted me, but I was terribly terribly tired. In the morning he told me my suspicions were true.

We made love then and I was able to keep the strangeness mostly at bay, but it still stayed with me to the point that my hair felt like someone else's, as if it were hanging down

over someone else's face. Outside the surf was pounding on the private beach of the yellow hotel, where the older lifeguard and his several sons patrolled its dazzling length.

The strangeness is really just a stillness where I am waiting.

And if I am not allowed to wait for some reason I become irritated, no matter what.

It would be better to leave me alone at those times; it's difficult for me

to wait without silence. But what

does the yellow hotel have to do with that? I think

something

        important
something
        intimate
something
        built in
something
        extremely pleasing.

And here is a geographical problem: Perhaps you are not going to the right mountain.
Perhaps the mountain you are going to is the easiest one to get to but not the best.
You will not take the time to go to the best place, why is that?
The nearby mountain is a mountain you have been to many times before.
So why do you think you will see something new there?

And I remember when I first met C and he kept saying *satisfying* all the time and I
think I asked him not to say it so often but now I understand.

He was having a yellow hotel.

He felt as if he were walking down those dark 1860's corridors lined with door after
door with high transoms and a rickety

hard-to-pull-the-lever

elevator

and he felt as if he were sitting on those endless wooden verandahs with the railings
painted white and he was reading a wonderful book perhaps even his own book
which he had just finished and he was watching

the pink-faced man in the blue shirt going down the steps very carefully holding his

little old sweet dog. It is (let me wait).

very satisfying.

I must say. And in many ways (I'm waiting) it is satisfying it is horribly satisfying
and also it's strange.

I feel as if I have read something strange.

A little like the metaphor that spat out mashed potatoes.

THE RECTANGULAR SLOT THAT GOES ALL THE WAY THROUGH THE EARTH

Just because you might not have realized you'd seen it does not mean it is not there. I was just about to drop something through it when a white dream awakened me.

The white dream that tasted vanilla
with a strange paste of mint.

I was about to drop something through there or perhaps fall through there, knowing that I might come out on the other side but that I could also be lost in space on the other side or burned up because I'd be traveling through

the red-hot core of the earth. There was a flat-top tree there in a luscious golden
green field and

I was alone.

Please do not ask me again to go see the parrots; I can't stand a bird in a cage.

Antonio Porchia said "The cold is a good counselor, but it is cold."

Very cold.

And twice on *The X-Files* characters use the precise words "deceive, inveigle, and
obfuscate."

I wonder if one could talk to one's uncle about that.

I require a lot of silence. How much?

Enough for the pigeons living in the abandoned buildings.

And what if I received an absolutely outrageous letter from A or B, saying all the things I imagine either of them to be thinking? Would that change anything?

A cut on the hand in the morning that vanishes before lunch. How are you supposed to believe a thing like that?

The pink becomes deeper if you look at it in a certain way.

Or even if you don't.

I am tired of my past and am creating a spot for resting.

Listening to C type, I think I have never heard anything so fast.

Then I listen to my own.

Fast also.

AIR FILLED WITH A CLOUD OF HAYSEEDS

Not hayseeds really, whatever they are, but something that looks the way *hayseeds* sounds.

the mystery of each body

you don't have any idea
really
how difficult it is to cut out the heart
to replace the heart with a heart
to replace the blood with air

you can't walk in someone else's shoes
if they don't fit you
or you can't take them off the other person's feet
because it's a cold day in january in seekonk new jersey

you don't understand about ingrown eyelashes
unless you have one
you can't pluck out what is not yours

don't be silly
each body each body each body
as unique as yours

as ignorant of yours

as plum

THE MYSTERIOUS REAPPEARANCE OF THE RUBBER CEMENT BOTTLE

Well you mustn't condescend patronize
though the temptation is there and tempered by *point of view*

Although I am convinced I've found evidence of unlawful entry and replacement
of the missing brown-red bottle of rubber cement
maybe it's just something I forgot I did myself *(oh la!)*

I can't say I really believe that but there is a glimmer of light coming under that
       door truly

and every door must be opened

eventually I guess *(the popular conclusion)*

And certainly there is much that can be done with typeface and much that can
       be done
with money

if you are fortunate enough to have both

I wouldn't count on it but you have to be able to recognize it if it happens

This morning the half-dying flowering plum *(October!)*
is covered with small red berries and half-dying leaves *(perhaps not* plum *at all oh la!)*
and also covered with magnificent starlings feasting on berries
Their spots and their funny-doll faces enchant me all day

The word *half* intrigues me enchants me all week it's true
since looking at the *l* and the *f* together is a continual challenge
and this applies even if they are capital letters (capital! *says the English person oh la!)*

Okay please stop saying *oh la* it was fun while it lasted

You know I'm still puzzled how the rubber cement bottle had a different label
when it reappeared

Did I imagine that also?

Did I imagine the .... also?
and the small objects (jewelry herbs eyeglasses) placed
next to the cat's bed under the bookcase?
and the flea circus the lovely pinkness the softness of your scalp
did I imagine that?

If so what power have I! Congratulations!

Lucky lucky
and in some ways it's going to be easier for me and in some ways harder

Fear of dependence or helplessness stemming from childhood experiences of not
being able to trust those upon whom you depended

That's not a sentence but you certainly understand it *(Kenneth Patchen come back!)*

Compassion for how people have learned to survive for example G whom we all
really like "but you can't take him anywhere"
He's liable to be an embarrassment

And the unexpected tenderness of Q's recent poems
and wanting to know the mysterious details it sounds like he had an affair
though that's none of my business

I imagined or dreamed someone said *Kenneth Patchen come back* and I think
it was J since he so loved Patchen
and I think he also said you didn't have to really read Patchen all the time you
        just had to cover yourself with the picture poems
and go softly to sleep

I'm going to make you notice me
I've been told I have a great attitude

Not by you

No I'm not angry I love your silly belt
Your socks are sweet your nose is pretty
You're going to get yourself in trouble soon though I think
I do it every day so I should know

IN THOSE DAYS PEOPLE LEFT THEIR KEYS IN THE CAR

He said "I've already got the prose poem thing down," and as he said that I saw a huge hawk fly right over the house holding a white mouse in its mouth. The mouse was from the lab in the city and the mouse called out "I prefer to die by hawk." He said "You're funny this morning," but I was weeping fat white tears for the mouse—or not for the mouse so much as for the hawk, who had caught a dread disease while stealing the infected mouse from the lab. He said "I cannot decide between the you you say you are and the you I want you to be," and I decided right then and there there would be no more talking. I grabbed him with my beak by the nape of the neck and twisted sharply. I smoothed back his fine white hair.

AS A HEART OF NEW PUSHED HARDNESS HOPES FOR MELTING

This morning it remains unclear
In another sense, in another time, a first man did not think
whether the crisis will be averted by continual assault
a second man "his type." (The wives
with imaginary or real medication of the preventive sort
of these two were friends.) This was not a romantic
or whether a visit will have to be made
assessment; rather, the first attempted to appease
to several tired physicians
what he felt to be almost an irrational need
of body and soul. The mind
on the part of him and his wife
does not seem to enter into it
to make sense of things. The second man
any more than it did yesterday
had accused the wife of the first
when she observed three men
of something untoward — they did not speak of it
constructing a fieldstone wall: one, highly muscled,
after the first discussion, wherein the second man
carting fieldstones from another pile
confronted the first man's wife with his, shall we say, unusual
closer to the second, who slathered each selection
idea. After that (and it was left
with a dollop of gray mortar, placing each
that the second man wasn't fully satisfied
atop the next with such extraordinary care
he was mistaken, although the wife made all valiant attempts
the mortar could not be seen from across the road — or even
to continue normally, except in her disgust
a few feet away — and the casual observer would begin to wonder
when the second man later offered his cheek to be kissed) nothing

whether the stones had simply fallen somehow
was spoken, except of course by the wife
into this wondrous heap, although of course that would never
to the first man, her mate, who was shocked and
seem true. The third man stood
dismayed. At first, however,
a little apart, watching with that careful attention
he was only surprised; it was later dismay set in,
that could only bespeak a hidden love. The second man, once
and he wondered whether some confrontation on his part
in a while, chipped off a corner of stone
shouldn't be initiated with the second man,
from a piece that did not quite fit. Then he went on. Clearly he did not care
whom unfortunately he had already somewhat
for one stone more than another. Perhaps no one
disliked. The first man's wife
had ever challenged this fairness
was truly valiant, as I have said,
of affection. Of course the stones would not ask, but the other
but suffered nonetheless, and she in her turn wondered
men might think to. I don't know. I don't
whether the second man had accused her in some attempt
pretend to understand it myself; I only know that the question
to separate the affections of her and her man, or even
raises others, others that clearly the three men had integrated
to come between her and the second man's wife, a treasured
into a highly successful, already existing palate of being,
confidant for years. No one else knew this had happened,
that served them well. They were themselves and they could see
and so advice was out of the question.
a correspondence between each stone, each air.

DARK HARBOR

"You can stand anything if you write it down."
Louise Bourgeois

At dinner in the seaside restaurant we had a long conversation, not rancorous, just thoughtful mostly, then afterward you said I looked so sad. A young couple went out the glass doors to the deck to look at the dark harbor, but they couldn't get back in, and I had to get up from the table and open the door. I waited too long, almost as if I wanted C to convince me it was the right thing to do, which was the same tenor as the conversation really. I made an excuse to them that there was a reflection on the door, but they were very grateful in any case and I probably need not have made it.

the night the sea
the night
the sea

The page is the page and there's no reason to try to make anything "leap off" it. Reading about Dubuffet's ghost/apparitions and also his amazing statement about how a picture or painting of a chair or even a poem or any verbal description of a chair is such a different thing from a sculpture of a chair because it is entirely possible that a person might try to literally *sit down* on a sculpture of a chair, confusing it with reality. Could I write a poem about a chair (or in which a chair appears) while I was entirely absolutely mystically practically spiritually psychologically *in touch* with myself so that someone would try to sit down in it?

All day C has been annoying me, although there's no good reason for it, my feeling annoyed that is. In the second restaurant (breakfast) he read the *Globe* about Gingrich resigning and he was happy, and I was happy to hear that also but happier to watch the parade of dogs and dog-walkers on Commercial Street in the early morning strained sun. Also although it's November I was curious about the Christmasy décor of the restaurant and wondered if it were like that year-round (i.e., having some significance for the owner) or if they simply started decorating for Christmas as soon as Halloween was over. Even the cotton café curtains had a pine-bough-ribbon-and-hanging-ball theme. Red and green.

Also a Dubuffet idea, that a "portrait" would probably have literally nothing to do with the physical reality of a person—rather it would be a depiction of a collection of subjective impressions made into visual (or literary?) form.

We walked out to the lighthouse and stood on the newly erected deck, which C informed me was made of a sort of recycled composite "wood." There was a steamer ship a long ways in the distance. I wonder about my sudden lack of direction (geographical) on this trip: decisions about right or left, east or west that I had easily been able to make in the past I have been unable to make correctly.

My new boots squeak uncontrollably; at first I thought I could fix the squeaking by putting some black electrical tape along the edges of the tongues and the eyelet holders, but it turns out anything plastic or plastic-like would squeak. The boots are deliberately not leather and are very very comfortable, so I will either figure something else out or learn to live with the squeaking.

I am comforted by supermarkets. When I am sad it seems to me that if the supermarkets are all right then everything is all right. I know this is shallow.

something woke me

it was you
standing in a dream
with your fist clenched
it was you

standing with your fist
clenched in a dream
making me amazed
shaking it in my face

something woke me
a train rushing by
a mile away
it was you

standing on the train
with your face clenched
shaking me amazed
awake a mile away

green dress, top button

1.

calm
falling
yellow
leaves

one by one by one by

must have been a frost last night said c

there must have been a landscape with real figures (animate & inanimate)
            among "unreal" shapes & forms

on tuesday november 17th i dream again of augusta the cat
of playing with her feet
many toes
and cirrus all between them

on thursday november 19th i dream of s
first time in months
this time seen only in a blue shirt from the back

hardly as threatening

i realize i must abandon all control
m mentions that too in the chinese bookstore

my favorite mechanical pencil is lost
so what will i call the new manuscript now
lobelia?

eclosion, the act of hatching from the egg

2.

m tries again to define *coincidence*
i wonder about writing a question-and-answer poem

i wonder about definitions
how one can define them
and still remain artless
modest
or even aspirated

my paternal grandmother i think used to talk about that

here is the windowsill: a windowsill is a place to hide flowers

here is a flowersill

place to hide windowpanes

window pain

if indeed you can see through someone

i understand *articulated* now: one can add or subtract

the red spiral spine of the notebook
anything less is a closure

3.

someone else in the house who has touched you but not nearby
that is peace

4.

x asked "what is sleep? why do you go away
from me? what
is sleep? why do you go a
way from me? what is
sleep?" z
was glad to go

i knew there would be trouble

this color is easier on the eyes

there can be just the tiniest bit of light in the room
that will not spoil it

please name this color

here is a black and white pen somebody gave me
perhaps the lawyer
i persuaded him to meet us at the house

5.

so many typos in this book:
"I saw myself in elationship to the stars"

a snow-covered figure
standing in front of a restaurant

i am searching for a noun
i have looked almost everywhere
when i find it the pain in my hip will go away

i will wear the green dress this morning with the loose top button

and not sew it yet

not even fool around

how we were happy in spain though you will not believe it

you just are never happy
you never admit to happy
you never choose happy
you are in love with your sorrow
your sorrow you say is clean
it's as filthy as a lie
even a snail is happy
sometimes
maybe always
a snail in its round happy house

even if you knew our friend h you would not be happy
for her tattoo
her tattoo the chinese character for tiger

if you had a beautiful spoonrest made of creamy ceramic and little blue fruits
sitting on your stove you would not like it
i don't know what kind of person this can be

lorca's dibujos make you happy
momentarily
inappropriately happy
you can like them because they are not yours
why don't you make your own dibujos
that's what you're really lusting after
but you will not do it
because it might make you happy

if you had a shetland pony on a daisy chain
you would find something to be sad about
even though the pony would be happy for the breaking of the chain
and walking along next to you of her own free will

if you washed your feet in a crystal cold canal
on a boiling hot day
on a mountainside in spain
and washed off all the dust red dust
i don't know if you'd be satisfied
or if you'd admit it

the blue the white of the water
the mountain town
the cobalt dome
the white white whitewash
the restaurant with the christ child in a pith helmet
the cat with the bent tail on the roof garden
the little cat who was happy in spite of her bent tail

many have thought it would take this to make you happy
or that
some have tried for years to get you to see it
or admit it
now in sorrow i see you're in love with your sorrow
even when sorrow rejects you and fate conspires
to make you happy

the great miro traded paintings for hats
near the green green river
because hats made him happy
near the green grey olive groves
and because his painting made the hatmaker happy
would picking almonds make you happy
as it made us very happy on the hillside
in guejar sierra
p's long smooth hand full of little almond fruits

talking and taking photographs with p and a

i don't think so
or at least you'd never admit it
you want us to admire your sorrow

to say your sorrow suits you
but sorrow suits no one no one

and the alhambra tiles and carvings
the salamanders and pools of the generalife
the fountain of the lions who look like tame dogs
half-tame cats climbing up up up to the top of the fountains to drink
the glazed ripe cherries
the small greenorange fruits

i have never even heard you exclaim over flowers
how is this possible
what about bee-balm
what about morning glories
roses like cabbage-heads big as our own

but i wonder if again i'm being too hard
if something has absconded with your happiness
even if you invited that something in perhaps you're not to blame
i don't want to be blaming the victim

or do i

the happiness (duende) happiness (passion) happiness (flowers)
of the baby-faced flamenco cantador
will never be yours

the chances of your sitting on top of one mountain and hearing the far-off goat bells
from another mountain
are slim
and you may never see the tiny trails of far-off goats as they trickle
in no formation whatsoever
down the face of the grey-green mountain
goats walking helter-skelter in a catlike way

when we rested during our walks through the alhambra i met a stray dog
a gentle little stray who was way too thin

who had sad yellow eyes
and he came to my hand
so gently
he sniffed my hand

i thought oh no he's hungry and offered him my cookie
the last of my cookie
a cookie i'd greatly enjoyed

and out of politeness or pity or simple good will he took it in his mouth
so gently
as if it were a communion wafer

i could *feel* his enormous gratitude
and something something else
the complications between us in that dry spanish air were enormous
i was not sure if it was his hunger or something else

then he laid it on the ground
with a sad and piercing carefulness

as if he couldn't bear to be happy

self-portrait with spoonrest

c says i am not the type who looks at a person and says oh you have arms and
         legs i love you
i'm hard to please
i don't think that's necessarily true

why is that little dog barking down the street
why doesn't somebody go see what's the matter
this puts me in mind of frost's little morgan in the snow
"whoever it is that leaves him out so late,
when other creatures have gone to stall and bin,
ought to be told to come and take him in"

thank goodness he stopped barking i was on my way down there

if i had a spoonrest i might be happy
i will have a spoonrest in the new house
an old stove and a spoonrest and pantry with glassed-in shelves
pink tiles in the bathroom upstairs and green downstairs
a breakfast nook (near the spoonrest) and a fine kitchen window where the
         spoonrest
can look out
on raspberries and mint and the old-fashioned hollyhocks that don't get rust
i will have mint there and a spoonrest
it is possible i will like more people
whether they have arms and legs or not
which actually has never been my standard

yesterdaymorning my brother told me a story
he said that after my father died and he (my brother) was ten years old
he'd bring tiny objects to the gravesite when we visited
and insert them in the earth near the headstone for my father to enjoy
one of these objects was a bullet
from one of my father's rifles
my father was a hunter a fact for which i've never forgiven him never will

and he was also a gunsmith and did many quite beautiful things with metal and
         wood
and in any case my then-little brother buried this bullet in the earth
and forgot about it for almost thirty-five years

then recently my brother went to visit my mother
who said the strangest thing had happened
she was planting those salmon-colored geraniums on my father's grave
and her trowel struck a hard object which turned out to be a bullet
an old bullet a crusty bullet
she put it on the table in front of my brother
who made an instantly sane decision not to tell my mother the story
for reasons we'd better not go into right here
and he said oh there's a lot of deer hunting goes on up there you know and she
         said well yes
but it certainly was a very strange thing
and my brother had to agree

then she told him she'd been sandpapering the end of the bullet to see if she
         could read the writing there
and he told her no! it's a live bullet
and you might set it off

she said how do you know it's a live bullet you haven't even picked it up yet

and he said he'd just assumed so

and so the subject was dropped but as my brother told me on the phone
         he's sure it hasn't been
dropped for good
he said it was one of those conversations where one person holds more knowledge
than the other but the other not only doesn't know about the subject but doesn't
         even have the vehicle in which to approach it

my grandmother had a spoonrest in the shape of a pansy

i wish i knew where to buy such a spoonrest
if anyone does please tell me right away

catenary

a word you cannot understand is a good word

use the word stone to build a wordhouse

as for catenary the curve a hanging flexible wire or chain assumes
when supported at its ends and acted upon by a uniform gravitational force the
        word *catenary* derived
from the latin "chain"
disproving galileo's long-endearing claim
that the curvature of a chain hanging under gravity would be a parabola

i'm glad galileo didn't understand it either
the curve is also called the alysoid and chainette
or *alysoid and the chainettes* a rock group from the 50's

who knows how this equation was obtained
or how gaudí dreamed his sweetcake castles upside-down all over it

in response to a challenge by bee-eaters in the sierras perhaps
that's all i can think of

yet the catenary and its chain and heavy bags
consumes me
as if my minimum surface suspended
over the cage of my life
would yield other lives other souls other outputs

if i were to become a curve

if i were to become a curve

the parametric equations for the catenary are given by

oh come on

the catenary gives the shape of the road (roulette) over which a regular
polygonal wheel can travel smoothly
the arc length, curvature, and tangential angle are

yes now you see

the slope is proportional to the arc length as measured from the center of symmetry
oh how beautiful

the slope is proportional to the arc length as measured from the center of
this bird who sings at 4 a.m. and 8 p.m. and whom we never see

its piercing clearnote song
a catenary of silence

see also calculus of variations, catenoid, lindelof's theorem, surface of revolution
and cite your references

refer to the tractrix and catenary in a book of curves
cambridge england cambridge university press if i recall correctly

pages 197 to 134 *(go figure)*

also the fabulous novel entitled mathematical snapshots not a novel at all some say
but i wonder
or the penguin dictionary of curious and interesting geometry
london 1991

a word you cannot understand is a good word

use the word stone to build a wordhouse
use the word house to build a stonehouse
use a catenary

pray to gaudí to understand it
ask him to forgive the train that killed him
fumble for your explanation of how this little word
is clearly as clearly as anything before

a bowl with a bag of white stars upside-down
in a deep blue navy blue sky

i saw the ghost

i saw the ghost and then you said that's a pear tree

i saw the wandering pawprints of the squirrel on the pear tree's trunk

i saw your lies masquerading as love in a wallet

i saw you put your hands over your mouth so you couldn't see me

i saw the pale ministry of snow and white bees land softly on your forehead

i saw you were not you that day

who were you
what will you find
i told you where to look for it
you looked puzzled

i dug up the grave of the man who loved animals
revived him
and put the hunter in his grave

if i had not ever seen you i would think you were a ghost

i would think you were shaped like a lighthouse

i would think your clothes were parts of your body
that could be taken off

i would bathe you in lavender

i would think you were so small
a mosquito might eat you whole

if i had never seen you

i have seen you
why do you look that way
who are you
when you're at home

do you avoid me because you've been forced to wear a hat

do you avoid me because you are wandering on the road's white line

i saw the ghost
i tell you i saw him
i saw the grey ghost flying right through the sky

a yard or so of flowered cloth

tacked up by one of the windows with a green background
something she might have made curtains out of
if they hadn't been looking for another apartment
and the angelhair fern in the bedroom which v said that must be your favorite
      thing and b said no it's dirty
and pointed to all the little leaf fragments littering the floor
and the huge space of wall above the tv b was saving for a sign he wanted to buy
from a retiring optician
his desire for the sign had made the optician suspicious
and now it was doubtful he'd sell or not easily
i asked b what he'd pay for the sign (a huge pair of old-fashioned eyeglasses)
      (oval lenses)
and he said that remains to be seen my dear that remains to be seen

b had recently been to the barbershop in town which was run by a once-famous
      singer from the 50's who now cut hair and called himself the snipper
and another time as he was walking out of another barbershop where the barber
      wasn't ever famous ever
the barber an old man shook b's hand and said you're my last customer now i'm
      retiring
i wasn't there but the way b described it made me feel as if i'd felt that barber's
      hand myself
sort of a soft hand
but strong
after 50 years or so of handling hair

love is a disease and an antibiotic and there is pain between the two and uncertainty
      before and after each

i have a vial of tears that belonged to nobody famous no saint no movie star
i found it in the subway
a place you can trust everyone

i will sprinkle them into my garden of false indigo
called truly baptisia
a cobalt blue color quite remarkable to see

last night she said i looked pale
all i knew was i was mad
there had been usurpation and denial
and there would be no good sleep

for sleep had been defined oddly and the weather report slipped down in bed
          between them
white lace curtains had been slit in half
hung up backwards and sideways
when i did it i said i knew what i was doing
and they looked quite beautiful

our friends who moved from framingham more than 20 years ago
have still one box in the basement that's never been unpacked
i'm in love with that box
and will break in their house to steal it

general do you understand love
snail on blade of grass do you
i don't understand even the slightest laws of nature
like how to get water to seek its personal best
and flow into the roots of plants directly without touching the ground

as humans we build tall houses but it does not make us taller

voices of the dinosaurs

1.

this world and all of its details could vanish

2.

i didn't know when to expect you or if to expect you at all
i had a feeling there was a cake in the garbage can
the voices of the dinosaurs haunt me in particular the wand-necked ones
i believe i have known them
i have listened to them gossip
is this some kind of lunatic conspiracy like the ones that say history never happened?
did someone say there were never any dinosaurs?

i've heard them singing alone and in chorus
sometimes like mockingbirds they imitate woodland sounds
some of them sound like monkeys although there aren't any monkeys yet
somehow they hear them

now that the floor is shiny in here the table legs rest on themselves
i don't think the room they made the dinosaurs stay in was even this large
i don't know who they is
but i know they were mistaken

i don't hear as much from you as i used to
the voice of your wristwatch was nervous and slow
like a wand-necked dinosaur a small one
today there are buds on the acacia but it's not yet spring
and someone will be disappointed before too long

we don't know where bridge street is
so we cannot cross over

3.

the voices of the dinosaurs committed the first opera
they had been well cast in a tragedy of hours
their voices woven in and out with fronds and ferns
and they died in the end like opera stars swooning
gazing into one another's eyes acknowledging eternity begetting no one

once again a bridge dream this time water sneaks up over the edge
and we wade in black shoes and acknowledge our eternity

my brother said a chamber-hearted dinosaur has been found

hard to believe it was no human's fault the dinosaurs died
hard to imagine they simply had to leave us when they left us
hard treatment of animals has left me suspicious
today's heavy rain has washed away the snow leaving rivulets
rain enough for dinosaurs
rain for the cock-robins yet to arrive
rain to forgive me

4.

use not roman numerals unless you are roman
does that orange "x" mean the tree is coming down
and what about the woman walking past it
we have a plant in a birdcage trying to get out i would love to cut the cage
my husband says no two giraffes' spots are the same
and that one of the first things he remembers learning
is that the human race could not survive without insects
last night a dream about a sea urchin and peter o'toole
nodder dolls we saw on the *antiques roadshow* fashioned after the beatles
and it struck me that in our minds we all have nodder dolls of those who've hurt us
and whenever the landscape trembles the little heads-on-springs begin to nod
and they nod and they nod and they trouble us a lot
i have dinosaur nodder dolls and they trouble me a lot
especially the wand-necked ones

wand-necked like guitars playing *wipeout* suddenly during a ballad
dinosaur fingers sliding expertly down the strings

5.

this world and all of its details could vanish

one man and one dinosaur obscure one another mysteriously
like a tire in a nail
i dream white wrought iron lawn chairs tipped over in the snow
as the dinosaurs are tipped
the architectural worries of the millions of dinosaur years
expanses of snow-covered ice on rivers
injured geese still feeding
dragging their broken wings like capes across the snow
mirrors melting like ice around sunny faces
i dream ceilings of the great gymnasiums hung with rows of inflatable boats
but no one is escaping

the dinosaurs' voices are long like water under water
these two branches long winched together are unhooked now by the wind

i dream of committing murder then of calling 911
because the victim isn't dead
or not as dead as my poor dinosaurs

6.

now that someone has tried to break in we know that the door lock works
the wand-necked dinosaurs move with the grace of camels
the grace of dinosaurs
what did they smell like—do they smell like lizards?
in other words a smell like mossy air
the dinosaurs tried to break into my dream
to tell me i am forgiven
the lecturer says our hands create empathy with the figure-drawing

because you always know where your hands are
i am old now and these children watch me write
those two branches are unhooked now over the water
and i dream of the water again and the dinosaurs who love me
the heads of dinosaurs high now on a dream of absent fear
still crave our alien hearts
we're not sure why they love us
their hands might have been the size of our hands
they might have just turned into hawks and flown away

7.

i'm not sure why you love me
in the snow everything can be seen so clearly the dinosaurs' luminescent green
blue yellow red and purple (for surely they were not brown were perhaps even striped
or chequered like cabs or dazzled in paisley)
against spiky black trees lemon air and wedgewood sky
this gift of a red-tailed hawk up close to the kitchen window
holds me in thrall and indeed i cannot move or i'll be seen he'll fly away
my husband says it is another visitation
yes you can read it this way it is not hard
this is the way your mind arises
a thousand kinds of sparrows maybe a slight exaggeration not too much
all at the feeder at the same time what is that grey-eyed bird what is that white one
i do see white
white against the white snow a white bird impossible yes impossible
must be white cloud snow flying
or the frosty breath of the dinosaurs

8.

a distortion in the window glass makes it look like squirrels leaping
in the blue spruces
i was sleeping when the fifteenth apple fell
and the groundhog we'd never quite forgotten went to sleep
in his plaid quilted jacket

o this world and all of its details could vanish
you've forgotten the intricate games you invented as a child
in your world populated by you and the dinosaurs
o i would like to tell you they are sleeping
and their voices are only silent through the dream that we are dreaming
i wish i didn't have to show you this crazy polaroid of the dinosaurs
in which they are fading away instead of fading into sight

a phone faintly ringing in the background

a call so unanswered a ghost
of an answering call